"Mix of hey that's poetry (uncanny resistance) with hey that's a text and smashing goals & fulfilling them along the way & saying my parents fulfilled them. Doing it differently being alive & an artist. I love this work. Unpredictable & sweet & strong to continue."
—EILEEN MYLES

"A thrilling punk rock epic that is a tour of all we know and can't admit to. Pico is a poet of canny instincts, his lyric is somehow so casual and so so serious at the same time. He is determined to blow your mind apart, and . . . you should let him."
—ALEXANDER CHEE

"A poet who will not hesitate calling out winter as a death threat from nature, Tommy Pico hears the wild frequencies in the mountains and rivers of cities. The marriage of extraordinary sharp writing with the most astute commentary on almost every possible thing a human will feel, think, do, dance like, or smell like. Then, suddenly, he asks, 'What if I really do feel connected to the land?' I read this book in one sitting. Then I read it in one sitting again the next day. The staying power of this poem I will blatantly say is without doubt!"
—CACONRAD

"The self-conscious labor of this poem explores a culture of asides, stutters, stammers, and media glitches. It's no wonder Tommy Pico manages to name and claim identity while also reminding us of his (and our!) limitlessness. *Nature Poem* is a book about our true nature."
—JERICHO BROWN

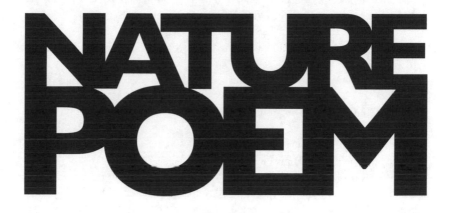

Published by Tin House, Portland, Oregon

Distributed by W. W. Norton & Company

Library of Congress Cataloging-in-Publication Data

Names: Pico, Tommy, author.
Title: Nature poem / by Tommy Pico.
Description: First U.S. edition. | Portland, Oregon : Tin House, 2017.
Identifiers: LCCN 2016056390 (print) | LCCN 2017010729 (ebook) |
    ISBN 9781941040638 (softcover : acid-free paper) | ISBN 9781941040645
Classification: LCC PS3616.I288 A6 2017 (print) | LCC PS3616.I288 (ebook) |
    DDC 811/.6—dc23
LC record available at https://lccn.loc.gov/2016056390

Second US Printing 2021
Printed in the USA
Interior design by Jakob Vala

www.tinhouse.com

NATURE POEM

TOMMY PICO

TIN HOUSE / Portland, Oregon

The stars are dying

like always, and far away, like what you see looking up is a death knell
from light, right? Light

years. But also close, like the sea stars on the Pacific coast. Their little
arms lesion and knot and pull away

the insides spill into the ocean. Massive deaths. When I try to sleep I
think about orange cliffs, bare of orange stars. Knotted, glut. Waves are
clear. Anemones n shit. Sand crabs n shit. Fleas. There are seagulls
overhead. Ugh I swore to myself I would never write a nature poem.

The sand is fine. They say it's not Fukushima. I feel fine, in the sense
that I feel very thin—I been doin Tracy Anderson DVD workouts on
YouTube, keeping my arms fit and strong. She says *reach, like you are
being pulled apart*

I can't not spill. Sometimes it, sometimes . . . what you see is what you
glut. There are sometimes insides.

I can't write a nature poem
bc it's fodder for the noble savage
narrative. I wd slap a tree across the face,
I say to my audience.

Let's say I'm at a pizza parlor
Let's say I'm having a slice at the bar this man walks in to pick up his
to-go order
Let's say his order isn't ready yet and he's chatty
Let's say I'm in Portland bc ppl don't tawlk to me in NYC
Let's say he's like, *meatballs are for the baby, pizza's for the little man,
Caesar salad's for the wife and the beer* he points to the beer and then
thumbs at himself, *the beer's for me.*

He has one of those cracked skin summer smiles

He keeps talking like I want to hear him
Like he's so comfortable
Like everybody owes him attention

I'm a weirdo NDN faggot

He puts his hands on the ribs of my chair asks do I want to go into the
bathroom with him

Let's say it doesn't turn me on at all

Let's say I literally hate all men bc literally men are animals—

This is a kind of nature I would write a poem about.

I don't like boys, men, or guys.

Don't like how they kick it on couches,
laid back, calves cocked

the neck muscles thrust up.

Don't like their dumb biceps bouncing the thunderclap laugh
choosing trucks over pink!? The musk the swoony wake, the misc
bulges, stupid weight training *Spot me bro*—

I was like *pfffft*, I says *yr kind of hard to miss?*

What they say to anyone ever in history, or in the locker room when they
think no one is listening in a tight towel. Or everyday when they expect
attention, ppl wide-eyed ears like satellites the words (apparently) torch
torchin to truth.

Don't like them tweeting, texting, um *peeling rubber wetsuits off in the
parking lot*

sweatpants no discernible underwear lookin like *whatever*

Or! When they slick back swab the deck pocket square shoulders—

The wave, the fade, the bang bangs.

Men dancing is fine tho.
Or like maybe men in socks? I dunno

I can't write a nature poem
bc I only fuck with the city
and my dentist is the only man who'll stick his meaty fingers
in my mouth rn. The office of my hummingbird heart rattles the
sparkling office.

It's okay, he says. *It's kind of . . . You'll hear when I clap my hands, but
you won't really care.*

Sooooo it's like gas-induced sociopathy?

Crickets.

He twists the knob

feeling bobs the biochemical

delta — care rolls out to sea. Cut off the head?

and a body can jerk for minutes afterward. Is life more than a
byproduct of nerves

crunch crunch heave have you ever eaten

rattlesnake? Not to be cliché, but it tastes like chicken. Everything
tastes like chicken, but then again I have shockingly little taste.

It's hard
feeling like a carcass bc u literally can't *feel*
like a carcass. You feel around instead.

I come around slowly, oxygen fuzzy dead bone spittle — a hole in my head.

Winter is a death threat from nature, and I don't respond well to predation—

it's not like summer, death in the form of barking men

takin issue w/the short shorts and the preen and the queenly holding hands

god forbid u step into the gnashing cold for a fizzy water and grapes, forget yr keys, the cell battery

dies n yr roommates out of town with their holiday families

plus mittens are dumb af

AND it's easy to fantasize abt snow when yr raised on the cusp of a desert—

Kumeyaay ppl aren't built for winter like metaphor—I mean metabolically and it happens, get this, it happens every. damn. year.

There's no exposure in Southern California,
no clanging heat in San Diego.
in LA? The snow comes in a can.

Cold was a curiosity, like rain. A ghost. No. A reanimation, a flourish of calendar art and novels with families in living rooms, huddled in a blizzard's fist.

We used the fireplace
for its smoky tang. When rains came from the eyelids of the sky, I cd feel the land licking the roof of its mouth. Hella satisfied.

Men smack

the monoliths in Mosul back to stone and dust. I'm devastated
in the midst of Vicodin
*Thank god for colonialist plundering, right? At least some of these
artifacts remain intact behind glass*, says History

Kumeyaay burial urns dug from context, their ashes dumped and placed
on display at the Museum of Man. Casket art, mantelpieces in SoCal
social well-to-do living rooms

A *warden is seldom welcomed*, I say.

Lives flicker, says History

I, too, wd like a monument, says Ego.

I'm abt to get fucked by Don Draper on a rooftop but stinging smoke
wraps us like thick blankets I wake up like *fuck did I have a cigarette
last night*, no dry sockets plz
but it's just my neighborhood on fire—I

rush outside the billow yanks across the sky and into Queens. It's an
archive burning, a record storage building near the water. Singed bits of
text rain onto the concrete, streets swallowed in fragments like a Sappho

How do statues become more galvanizing than refugees
is not something I wd include in a nature poem.

Captive and being returned to the wild
captive breeding and release program

Marius the giraffe put down by his handlers at Copenhagen Zoo,
dissected in front of patrons and fed to the lions

literally fed to the lions

in 2014

child slaves sleeping on fishing nets in Somalia, in Bangkok

OkCupid asks what's worse—a starving child or a starving dog, and
I'm like *is this a fucking joke?*

Dragonflies experience a kind of quantum time, see a much richer
spectrum of colors like a range of snowcapped mountains on molly and
mushrooms and sherbet watercolors

and I'm supposed to believe *we're* such miracles?

Ray Rice punches his girlfriend unconscious on camera and drags her
out of the elevator, and I'm supposed to give a fuck about pesticides?

That's not a kind of nature I would write a poem about.

Janjaweed, the Lord's Resistance Army, Al-Shabaab, Boko Haram, Oscar Pistorius, the Tea Party, Andrew Jackson, the Niña the Pinta and the Santa Maria

WHAT'S YR NATIONALITY!?!? This guy shouts at me during drag queen karaoke at this gay bar two stops down the line.

In order to talk about a hurricane, you first have to talk about a preexisting disturbance over the ocean, so you have to talk about mean ocean temperature, so you have to talk about human industry and sun rays, so you have to talk about helium, so did you know helium was named for the sun god Helios and was defined by a gap in the solar spectrum so literally not itself but what surrounded it, so of course we have to talk about the solar system, the Milky Way, the networks of universe and the Big Bang.

How far back do you have to go to answer any question about race?

UM, AMERICAN? I say

or

KUMEYAAY. I say *I'M FROM THE KUMEYAAY NATION,*

which are both technically true, but I know that when he says NATIONALITY he's saying *you look vaguely not like a total white boy* plus I'm trying to get lucky, so I put on my face that's the opposite of a tall can tipped over and glugging out onto the floor

I'M FROM AN INDIAN RESERVATION NEAR SAN DIEGO I burst back, over the drag queen sort of singing the Michael Bublé version of "Feelin Good."

When James hugs me hello

he stoops

(bc he is very tall)

nuzzles his forehead into the hook

of my neck

takes a big, long *sniff*

growls soft and low.

James is a stone

cold

dummy. But when he does *that*?

If this was an 80s hair band music video

I wd totally groupie

toss my frillies onto the stage of James.

Dear Gays,

I wish yr attention span was as "athletic"

as yr bod

The world is infected

Systemic pesticides get absorbed by every cell of the plant, accumulate in the soil, waterways

kiss the bees

knees, knees (in a Guns N' Roses way)

goodbye.

The world is a bumble bee

in the sense that, *who cares?*

My thumb isn't terribly green but it's terribly thumbing at me

it seems foolish to discuss nature w/o talking about endemic poverty which seems foolish to discuss w/o talking about corporations given human agency which seems foolish to discuss w/o talking about colonialism which seems foolish to discuss w/o talking about misogyny

In the deepest oceans

the only light is fishes—

luciferin and luciferase mix ribbons flutter in the darkness

i am so dumb thinking about this makes me cry i am so dumb

Dear NYC:

The only thing viral about Ebola is the Internet.

oh, but you don't look very Indian is a thing ppl feel comfortable saying to me on dates.

What rhymes with, *fuck off and die?*

It's hard to look "like" something most people remember as a ghost, but I understand the allure of wanting to know—

Knowledge, or its approximate artifice, is a kind of equilibrium when you feel like a flea in whiskey.

I used to read a lot of perfect poems, now I read a lot of Garbage

by A. R. Ammons

the old mysteries avail themselves of technique.

It's disheartening

to hear someone say "there's no magic left" bc I love that YouTube of Amy Winehouse singing "Love Is a Losing Game" at the Mercury Prize Ceremony and yesterday I overheard that Brooklyn means "Broken Land"—there aren't many earthquakes in the city, but there's the fault line of my head.

Pain is alienating, but blue breath breaking on a voice is the magic that makes ppl believe.

What, I learn to ask, *does an NDN person look like exactly?*

This white guy asks do I feel more connected to nature
bc I'm NDN
asks did I live *like in a regular house*
growing up on the rez
or something more salt
of the earth, something reedy
says it's hot do I have any rain
ceremonies

When I express frustration, he says *what?* He says *I'm just asking* as if
being earnest somehow absolves him from being fucked up.

It does not.

He says *I can't win with you*
because he already did
because he always will
because he could write a nature
poem, or anything he wants, he doesn't understand

why I can't write a fucking nature
poem.

Later when he is fucking
me I bite him on the cheek draw
blood I reify savage lust

I'm telling YOU all about ME

In order to prove OUR intelligence, OUR right to live, WE becomes I

a distinct note above the cacophony of the land and the animals and the scar tissue running across the gauntlet of the sky

I have to pee so fucking bad

I tell my singing teacher.

I tell Roy that since I been taking singing lessons, it's harder to hold it in. The fill of breath and the body's fist jabbing forward—

So, if I wait? I'm going to piss my pants.

I am the opposite of pee shy.

Do you remember Fergie? Do you remember when Fergie peed on stage? In San Diego?

Okay, jeez go to the bathroom, she says.

Even minor snaps I cast a srs argument.

My singing teacher tells me *find your center*

Tornado fucking is a natural phenomenon

wherein you start on your stomach,

get flipped to the right side,

then he slides under you slams

u into his hips, both in a sort of crab walk flip left

before returning to (yoga term) stomach pose.

When me n James fuck around the house, we fuck *around*
the house.

That's some Shame *shit*

says my roommate after I dusk back from Adam's
after waking up with James
spending the afternoon at Ryan's place.

No Jess, I'm a faggot on a Saturday

Gay men are the worst people ever

bc if they don't want to fuck you,

you are nothing to them.

Yet they love dogs.

"Malibu" by Hole is one of the greatest songs in America

when I was younger I thought it was a sexy like summer story abt the
sandy aesthetic wonder of a SoCal summer beach town

How you listen to something completely in yr own head.

and it does sort of function in that pop anthem sense, but maybe
now as an adult w/an inured understanding of shorthand, addiction's
weather-beaten features, and who quite frankly has felt the reluctant love
you sometimes can't even look at

now I understand it's a plea
to get someone famous into rehab—
Malibu, a destination for the famously fucked up
We're all watching you. You know what to do.

It's biblical, submit to the angels and Part the sea
to yr freedom
but the object is swallowed

Songs r spells
like poems

imagine casting one to drive the lover dry
Creating a sublime hook
a thrall of fandom in its wake
Yet the mate remains eternally unsaved

Last night I had a dream that I was a ghost who gave blowjobs and that is pretty much the experience of dating in the city

When I say I'm having catfish banh mi

what I mean is leave me alone
what I mean is I love candy but I'm an adult I only let myself have
candy at the movies
so I've been goin to the movies A LOT

Sometimes on dates I buy the box of gold bears but keep them
scrunched in the cup holder on the arm rest bc I don't want him to
think I'm the kind of adult who still hoovers candy (by which I mean
I don't want to b the kidn of adult who still hoovers candy) but fuck
I still bought them like in good fun was gonna offer him some but
he doesn't like sweets and I thot too long abt the prospect of box of
gummies breach n we been kind of cuddlin so the flick is halfway
over all those other snacky losers finished their soppy nachos or r just
wrapped in the movie like a normal person n it's waaaaay past the
crinkling hour but HALLE-FUCKING-LUJAH he has to pee so I
quick rip the shit like a bird neck eat a handful of gummy bears shove

the box back in my backpack before he gets back NBD crisis

averted earth

a golden orbit of simplicity.

My primary device is personification, says Nature. *Do your associations consider my mercurial elements?*

Nature is kind of over my head

the speech sweeps inland is overtaking

Nature keeps wanting to hang out, and I've been looking for an excuse to use the phrase "hackles of the night" but you can't always get what you want.

Every date feels like the final date bc we always find small ways of being extremely rude to each other, like mosquito bites or deforestation

like I think I'm in an abusive relationship w/nature

then again I think I'm in an abusive relationship w/myself, I whisper after pinching my squishy belly

but for reals I leave yr apt in the early train of my hangover thinking *that was a weird bump* like all jostled but back on the open road

then like clockwork u txt two days later sayin, greetings from the Pines—you free Tuesday night?

and I'm both charmed and suspicious, which is probably redundant, and also the soil of my landscape and a landing strip.

I don't like thinking abt nature bc nature makes me suspect there is a god.

Monumental bowl of ash overtaking hikers, for example — the cloud's arms sweep down the mountainside

a gasp from the mouth of natural wonder, eyes peel toward the sky

like memory

Agreed. A greed. Aahhh. Greed.

God wants everything, n I'm like *God — you, I'm sorry, but you are too much of a time commitment. I have a work thing. It's not you, it's me.*

God is wearing short shorts and demands worship, n I'm like *God, yr balls are showing!!!*

I'm trying to explain this very slowly.

My friend Jesus works at a dispensary. In the waiting room, they have one of those ball lightning things. Plasma globe. Makes everyone feel like Storm. Whatever keeps stoners staring

is the only kind of nature I could bear.

We are the last animal to arrive in the kingdom—even science will tell you that.

My father takes me into the hills we cut sage. He tells me to *thank the plant for its sacrifice, son*. Every time I free a switch of it a burst of prayer for every leaf.

I'm swoll on knowing this? Sharing the pride of plants

My mother waves at oak trees. A doctor delivers her diagnosis.

When she ascends the mountains to pick acorn, my mother motherfucking waves at oak trees. Watching her stand there, her hands behind her back, rocking, grinning
into the face of the bark—

They are talking to each other.

I am nothing like that, I say to my audience.

I say, *I went to Sarah Lawrence College*

I make quinoa n shit

Once on campus I see a York Peppermint Pattie wrapper on the ground, pick it up, and throw it away. *Yr such a good Indian* says some dick walking to class. So,

I no longer pick up trash.

I want to be the one who eats the candy
at the Felix Gonzalez-Torres exhibit, not the one splashing his face
with cold water in the bathroom

but we r who we r

like jambalaya.

Let's say I was raised on television and sugar and exhausted parents
working every job that poked its head from the tall grasses of opportunity

who didn't go to college but still read poetry to each other and wrote
songs and made sculptures and read law documents at the beach while I
threw like seaweed on my cousins
but opportunity to what?

My current envy list includes ppl who make decisions, in general.
Envy is a shit tit. I meet a boy and I miss him. Time, a paragon of
confidence, taps me on the shoulder and asks

if I get legit anxiety when someone calls from a number I don't know,
cos it's like—who still calls?

I've always wanted to know, I say, *why they call you Father*

You can't reflect and decide at the same time. If language is a structure
born of the desire to communicate, can I really be blamed when
Money says *anxiety is only real when the face breaks* and I'm chipping
like paint?

I shoot thru yr stupid sky like a stupid sky

You are like the third convertible in a row or like seafoam socks in the
fat far rockaways

I can't look you in the eye and listen
at the same time. Yr not stupid at all, you say things like "the skin of
art," but here with me in the back of this margarita—you must be very,
very stupid

Ppl here wear stupid shirts that button all the way up to the top of the
tower, and inevitably fall

I look too much into the mirror of my worst self
so life feels like always breakin in a pair of new shoes
and my hunch is we'll be naked soon having sex like those handsoaps
that smell like parsley sort of refreshing but chemical Nothing like the
real thing n you wd prolly notice if we fucked with all my clothes on
bc yr of course so hazel
and stupid.

Nothing can fall that wasn't built

except maybe my self-esteem bc I have a hunch that I was born with it
intact but then America came smacked
me across the face said *like it*
n the sick thing is getting smacked across the face makes me so wet rn

and that's prolly why poetry, bc in order to get inside
a poem has to break you
the way the only thing more obvious than your body
is leaving yr shirt on in the pool.

The perigee moon haloes the white comforter in a Beyoncé way.

You shine like a bar of soap in the shadows.

The perigee moon is above both of us, in Portland, in NYC, in San Diego, in Hong Kong, Abu Dhabi, Guaynabo, Sri Lanka

Knowing the moon is inescapable tonight

and the tuft of yr chest against my shoulder blades—

This is a kind of nature I would write a poem about.

Everyone is looking for their stupid soulmate rn

Sade likens dating to war, says she's *on the front lines*

which is also a kind of hunger. Really, I just see teeth

or a desert—u know yr thirsty
when you wonder *does the bartender think I'm cute, or is he tryin to get
a tip?*
but that's the wilds for you.

Everyone wants to know where can they meet a good guy
then wants to go to a gay bar on Saturday night.
I'm cool with contradictions, but don't lie to yrself—

Hope
is a charred skeleton
of a house visible from a road that snakes
through the valley of memory
where fig trees burst from the ground like throaty laughter.

Winter, like thirst, is one of nature's ultimate burns
implicit in which is the analogy of touching a hot stovetop.

I'm tired of astrology and bffs
saying *Find the spring*
bc spring is an asshole, getting yr hopes n temps up then plunging like
self-esteem. Plus it's nearly half-terrifying to show again the sea of my body

and yet

I like the way my head shivers
restin on yr stomach when you say *If I keep hanging out w/u I'm gonna get a six pack*
from laughing.

Like poison oak or the Left Eye part in "Waterfalls"
you become a little bit of everything you brush
against. Today I am a handful of raisins and abt 15 ppl on the water taxi.

When my dad texts me two cousins dead this week, one 26 the other
30, what I'm really trying to understand is what trainers @ the gym
mean when they say "engage" in the phrase "engage your core"
also "core"

restless terms batted back and forth.

Rest is a sign of necrosis. Life is a cycle of jobs. The biosphere is alive
with menthol smoke and my unchecked voicemails. I, for one, used to
believe in God
and comment boards

I wd say how far I am from my mountains, tell you why I carry
Kumeyaay basket designs on my body, or how freakishly routine it is to
hear someone died

but I don't want to be an identity or a belief or a feedbag. I wanna b
me. I want to open my arms like winning a foot race and keep my
stories to myself, I tell my audience.

Grief is sneaking cigs from the styrofoam cups on the tables next to the
creamers and plates of Mary's pineapple upside-down cake, running off to
the playground behind the schoolroom trailers to (try and) smoke them

We were supposed to grow old together, hold down food, run for cover, give birth.

Body the job
was to keep breathing.

the fabric of our lives #death
some ppl wait a lifetime for a moment like this #death
reach out and touch someone #death
he kindly stopped for me #death
kid-tested, mother-approved #death
oops, I did it again #death
it keeps going, and going, and going #death
I'm lovin it #death
because you're worth it #death
the best a man can get #death
maybe she's born with it #death
a whole new world #death
high, flying, adored #death
be all that you can be #death
It's . . . Alive!!! #death
the freshmaker #death
stick a fork in me #death
when you've got it, flaunt it #death
why you gotta be so rude #death
the best part of wakin up #death
it's morphin time #death
hello, is it me you're looking for? #death
just do it #death
Got #death
he can get it #death
what's the 411, son #death
takes a lickin and keeps on tickin #death
hang in there, baby #death
mr. big stuff, who do you think you are #death

solid as a rock #death
all day, every day #death
rude boy #death
yr givin me fever #death
that's the way love goes #death
almost doesn't count #death
hosted by Neil Patrick Harris #death
yr not the boss of me #death
clever girl #death
o say can u see #death
shots shots shots shots shots shots #death

AngelNafis: 'Do Right Woman' is literally a church pew. #Aretha

heyteebs: I can't even hear the first three notes of that intro w/o getting misty

AngelNafis: it's basically mathematics. Aretha plus a person having any sliver of a soul whatsoever equalz holy-feelz.

heyteebs: gaia is alive in those pipes

AngelNafis: LOL listening now im almost stressed out by what an opposite of an alien she is. not from outerspace but rather, THE CORE OF EARTH

heyteebs: can I reproduce this twitter convo in nature poem plz

AngelNafis: only if u eulogize me when I DIE SHORTLY AFTER

heyteebs: Don't Play That Song 70s TV version is basically an argument for thermodynamics

AngelNafis: 'Call Me' is to be played at my funeral/graduation/birthday cake cutting ritual/baptism/when i walk down the aisle

AngelNafis: listening to it right now and am more river than a river

heyteebs: omg this is a song abt friendship all the YOUs, but cd also b a polyamorous anthem?

AngelNafis: the thought of a polyamorous anthem EXHAUSTS me. FRANDS it has to be.

heyteebs: Do Right Truth

if the spark is elemental
if the phase changes

the first thing we noticed was your eyes your big eyes looking right at us

if infusing the valley with yrself
if light is over
whelming
if a crumple of heavy human in the careful hair

the birds I forgot abt the birds says auntie out from lockup

if vapor
if the carapace

the universe whirs its ghost of TV snow

if I pick my nose
if I see a flannel
if I was your girl
all the things I'd do to you

I'm going to be so sad when Aretha Franklin dies.

Stars are characters
in the tome of the night sky, which I shd work more at deciphering but no
I'll just sit here and think abt the sequel to A *Beautiful Mind* I just
invented called A *Ugly Bag*

and literally can't stop giggling to myself in the cool quiet office like
it's bad like it's a high school math test someone farted situation

Tracing shapes in the stars is the closest I get to calling a language mine:

The Ripening Mango. Three Snaps in a Z Formation. Amy Winehouse.

Naming is basic and audacious, a claim

My ideal power-couple name is TomCula bc I'm pretty sure that
ancient horror faggot could get it, plus I'm into upward mobility, know
my way around caskets, and wd love to mist myself thru doors

I sit in the cool quiet office and invent myself some laughs in an
attempt to maneuver from a sticky kind of ancestral sadness, bein a
NDN person in occupied America, and the magic often works

until I think *why is it so damn hard to spell maneuver* and *why does it
always look wrong* my great grandparents had almost no contact
with white ppl like the shutter of a poem is the only place where I can
illusion myself some authority

Everyone remembers the weather when discovering a body.

I think it's perfectly natural to look skyward.

Body

All of yr flecks, flakes n gurgles? Ew.

I sweat. I tell myself it's just what bodies do.
I have chicken fingers for breakfast.
My cousins have cirrhosis.

Body

I am not my body. Get me out of here.

When you grow up around funerals, you learn pretty quick a body in
a casket is bloated but somehow still sunk—A waxy calm. Where was
the person who'd gone

My family was like a reservation *Six Feet Under*—parents sang the old
Spanish songs, Kumeyaay birdsongs, church songs, led prayers at every
NDN funeral from here to Yuma. Gila Bend. Tucson. "Funeral" was
the first game my brother played. I'd turn to my cousins wonder which
of us wd make it to old age.

Watch him take their feelings, said mom in the hospital waiting room
as my father held hands with the weeping family. He slowly bent into
the grief above them, spoke on the dead and began weeping, too. *Now
watch,* she said, *how relieved the room gets.*

Even some jokes? He stays heavy tho
Her voice, a sail in the darkness.

Revulsion, I thought, was abt self-esteem but now I think might be a warning.
Solution to the problem of having a body.
Body: *don't get too attached to me*

Science predicts we'll discover alien life by 2025
Dudes' legs on the subway are constantly spreading

Nature asks aren't I curious abt the landscapes of exoplanets—which, I
thought we all understood planets are metaphors
like the Vikings, or Delaware

The night sky yawns over the city, indistinct
but for the spell
Miss Night Sky of my childhood was darkest toward the desert, where her
features chill and sparkle and swoon with metal
lighting up the dark universe
I wanted to stop looking up and start marching forward
like a metaphor

NDN teens have the highest rate of suicide of any population group
in America. A white man can massacre 9 black ppl in a church and be
fed Burger King by the cops afterward. A presidential candidate gains a
platform by saying Mexican immigrants are murderers and rapists

It's hard for me to imagine curiosity as anything more than a pretext
for colonialism

so nah, Nature I don't want to know the colonial legacy of the future.

Let's say I'm coiled by the part in the Al Green song "Love &
Happiness" after the toe-tap beginning when the guitar twang lifts a
musk of *mmmmgh* into the air

Let's say you're talking to me when this happens and yr feelings bruise
but I literally can't

hear you
and in fact I *no, no* my finger to yr face when you

or that drop in "Mine" by Beyoncé where she says "no rest in the kingdom"

(note to self: write pop song called "Once, Twice, Three Times Beyoncé")

the shreds of Al's voice Bey's deep gauze stuffed deep in my like chakras

I have the vague feeling in the thoroughfare of my thought process

like I care what yr saying ghostly

recognition of the fact that yr getting insulted, but srsly? Give me

a minute.

This absence of reason—but a flood that feels reasonable to me—is this
I wonder is this, *natural*?

or does music turn me into a sociopath?

My roommate Danny says music makes you gay, but only some ppl
realize this is happening.

Let's say I want to get a nose piercing.

Let's say I'm 30 years old.

Let's say nothing big and bull-like, nothing too attractive, nothing chandeliering from septum to lobe. Just a simple, little stud nothing more.

Is it normal to get a nose ring at 30?

Normal is defined not by what it is, but what surrounds it. Meaning it could literally be anything, and is nothing.

Is it normal to get a nose ring at 30?

No, it's not.

Am I just afraid of death?

Yes, probably.

Is there nothing more normal than fearing death?

It is very natural to fear death.

Should I get a nose ring?

It would look very cute on you.

My family's experience isn't fodder
for artwork, says Nature in btwn make outs

But you'll drink yourself to sleep?

Who is the "I" but its inheritances—Let's play a game

Let's say Southern California's water is oil

Let's say Halliburton is the San Diego Flume Company
and I am descended from a long line of wildfires
I mean tribal leaders

The Cuyamaca Flume transported mountain runoff and river water into
the heart of San Diego. Construction began illegally, in secret, in the
1880s. The creek bed dried. The plants died. The very best citizens of
San Diego called it "deluded sentimentality" to give Indians any land or
water. As if these are *things*, stuff to be owned or sold off

I am missing many cousins, have you seen them?

The sadness is systematic. Suspicion is the lesson that sticks. I forget

When Pio was young, he tended sheep. The flock numbered a couple
thousand strong, and he herded them across the four corners of San
Diego County

Drought makes us restless, searching for nourishing territory

Ventura kept horses. He used them to ferry NDN ppl across the county's mountain trails, like the first reservation taxi driver. You cd say that, like his father, Ventura had a flock. They both went on to become chiefs

Sometime much later comes me

I scout from the peak
of our sacred mountain
I'm dragged to the center
of town in chains
I'm old women scattered
along the creek
my little hands squeeze
my little mouth shut
drawn into nooks
within the valley
like a sharp breath
while shaggy men on horseback
following the water
seek brown bodies
for target practice strong
brown backs for breaking
in the name of the church
Valle de las Viejas
blue echoes split
the early evening They spit
and ride on
but I keep my breath in

Cahuillas and Kumeyaays often banded together in the borderlands
of Northern San Diego, esp post-contact. The name "Pablo" crosses
both sides of our tribal lineages like a stitch. I've read they're very good
at *peon*, a game of predicting the banded patterns of black & white
painted bones

Somehow other ppl know all the rules
of dating—Def do NOT send him that txt, Jess says
I wish more of my young self was free to learn abt flirting
and the Whitney Museum and the Shirelles
instead of which halls not to walk down for fear of getting my faggot ass
beat or what to do when yr cousin high on crystal points a gun at you

but here we are at the cap of this party, sitting across a kitchen table
getting hot drinking from the bottle. Yr the ghost of horror. I mean gust.
I mean boner. I mean I'm new

at likin you. Generally.

You move. My move. Your move. My move.

I forget

the issue was citizenship. William Pablo became a figurehead of NDN
resistance in the north: do our tribes remain independent—isolated
on small reservations in the foothills and mountains—or descend to
the city and assimilate into the general population?

The "You" consumes so sweetly
We forget the game ends.

People r so *concerned* abt "the Earth"
in the sense of kale salad and bruised
gin

She'll be just fine. We might not make it, hopefully. We'll exhaust
ourselves soon what with global population blooms and San

Loco macho nachos and ruddy from frozen margaritas you reach for
my arm. *You drifted off again.* You ask, *What are you thinking about?*

What the hell happened to INOJ

What are you all on, Radiolab is so fucking boring and white
noise That naked emperor

We're chemists, but it's not a science. Science is pretty racist, but
inventions reflect their creators

keep living

keep living

keep living

there was an orchard in the valley. Sand Creek was shrinking. This
is all very blurry to me. Candelaria gathered wild food from the hills
and woods. She tamed the intrusion of Spanish crafts, made *pinole*—a
blend of native seeds and Spanish barley. She churned butter and
made lace. She ground acorn in ancient *metates* and wove baskets
from dry grasses

We're at San Loco bc that's what I wrote

I was just thinkin The Last Supper *says way more abt Da Vinci than it does abt the good book, you know? There's no likeness for the apostles— those were just men about his life or something. Who is Jesus in the painting but the painter? Or is he the Judas?*

Just kidding I never think.

James looks at me like I'm not speaking English. *I believe in facts*, he says. He says, *you talk like you're always being interrupted by yourself.* He says, *you always take big breaths before you speak, like an excited child.*

Gulp.

What is a fact even?

James rolls his eyes. *What do you mean what's a fact? A fact is a fact. Facts are real. Proven. Objective.*

like restaurants in a changing neighborhood

a straight guy saying "size queen"

white gay saying "GO OFF"

Kelly Clarkson singin w/ En Vogue that part in "Free Your Mind," *oh lord forgive me for havin straight hair, it doesn't mean there's another blood in my heir*

Don't get me wrong—I literally love Kelly Clarkson. Things reflect their intersections.

I say *Facts are fallacies, created and curated by authority figures w/ agendas* and I say, *Facts are used to subjugate, intimidate, enslave, and kill entire "races" of ppl reproductive rights etc* I say, *so yeah I have a complicated relationship with facts and pretty much everything. The only thing objective abt facts is yr blind allegiance to them. James.*

or, I say nothing cos I'm tryin to get lucky.

I can't write a nature poem bc English is some Stockholm shit,
makes me complicit in my tribe's erasure—why shd I give a fuck abt
"poetry"? It's a container

for words like *whilst* and *hither* and *tamp*. It conducts something of
permanent and *universal* interest. Poems take something like an apple,
turn it into the skin, the seeds, and the core. They talk abt gravity, abt
Adam, and Snow White and the stem of knowledge.

To me? Apple is a NDN drag queen who dresses like a milkmaid and
sings "Half-Breed" by Cher

I wd give a wedgie to a sacred mountain and gladly piss on the grass of
the park of poetic form
while no one's lookin

I wd stroll into the china shop of grammar and shout *LET'S TRASH
THIS DUMP* then gingerly slip out

and unrelated, once I called a cab to take me thru the drive-thru @
White Castle after the dining room closed

I sob

at a Tim Dlugos that Roy is reading me at the vegan diner on the
formerly Italian side of Grand Street. *This is OUR medium*, he says.

My grandmother dreamed of Tin Pan Alley and wrote a song once
with the chorus "Your kisses drop like atom bombs"

Get in, loser—we're touring landscapes of the interior. In the mist

of words: the plume the matter the radiant energy

feeble   defective   inferior   imbecility   pure deviant

 American   mixed   basic   standard   data crazy facts

moron   intelligent classic   good   unfit fit   sane

        masc

open   chill   smooth   fun   educated   artsy well-

traveled   laid   back   cool   quirky   quality

        toned   agenda-free gifted   nice   professional athletic

        secure   facts down-to-earth   mild-to-wild   that

spark   the x-factor my truth   flesh tone   support our troops she's

crazy that's amazing natural   normal   perfect

you know what I mean?

I have chosen—you have chosen—he or she had chosen—we have chosen—they have chosen

whose origin word, *cēosan*, meant something more like to taste or to try, "only remotely related to choice"

an illusion of capitalism, like control

Ppl often look unfazed by Kenyan university massacres and the onslaught of James Franco. Behavior is mutable. Mirrors love attention.

Like everyone,

I read a Choose Yr Own Adventure w/my fingers keepin tabs on various forks in the text, to backtrack when reachin a dead end

How often do you choose hunger, or cheese burger? A space in btwn is hard to see when you're all borderlands—

We're on the rooftop of the Wythe Hotel. It suggests exposure. It shoots up like teeth, the cool breeze sobering like a newly sober ex

turning softly into peaches from the light behind the bottles

He cups my neck (you hate all his friends) The hairs on his face like an English garden (his sister's a racist) Taller than I remembered (he played you like a dolly then tossed you aside c'mon TEEBS)

carrying

the past in oneself, like a word

Language is engineered so naturally it's like it doesn't even happen

a shifty pigeon
eyes my sub sandwich

adaptive as progress, the grey city—it fevers me.

Language tells the story of its conquests, its champions, its admixtures,
while moving onward into new vessels: Lupin the cat waddles to his
water bowl.

Language often fails me, the static cling of an unknown word and the
urge to be heard
but also
the full freakin phrases that are somehow a dry barrier to others like,
black lives matter, or *rape culture*, or *"spirit animal" suggests indigenous
religion and spirituality is ridiculous*

Linguists say a language is dead when its only speakers are adult, that
in a hundred years 90% of the worlds languages will be kaput

A melody.

A lyric.

A cave.

A blue orbit suggested by echoes.

lol the word of the day on dictionary.com is *diddle*.

I will always be alone.

Here is a short, peaceful, pastoral lyric:

Crappy water
Shoots thru purgatory creek
On its way to the Colorado River

My bad, says the EPA after accidentally dumping 3 million gallons of
waste in the stream.

Fuck you too, says Nature.

Onstage I'm a mess
of tremor and sweat
I must have some face-blindness? bc I can't tell the difference btwn the
faces
of attention and danger

The gift of panic is clarity—repeat the known quantities:

Today is Wednesday.

Wednesday is a turkey burger.

My throat is full of survivors.

Science says trauma cd be passed down, molecular scar tissue, DNA
cavorting w/war and escape routes and yr dad's bad dad

I've inherited this idea to disappear
Oh but you're a natural performer

In the mid 1800s, California wd pay $5 for the head of an NDN and 25¢
per scalp—man, woman, or child. The state was reimbursed by the feds

When yr descended from a clever self adept at evading an occupying
force, when contact meant another swath of sick cousins, another
cosmology snuffed, another stolen sister

and the water and the blood and the blood and the blood and the
blood and the blood

u flush under the hot lights

I can't write a nature poem bc that conversation happens in the Hall of
South American Peoples in the American Museum of Natural History

btwn two white ladies in buttery shawls as they pass a display case of
"traditional" garb from one tribe or another it doesn't really matter to anyone

and that word *Natural* in *Natural History* hangs
also *History*
also *Peoples*
hangs as in frames

it's horrible how their culture was destroyed

as if in some reckless storm

*but thank god we were able to save some of these artifacts — history is so
important. Will you look at this metalwork? I could cry —*

Look, I'm sure you really do just want to wear those dream catcher
earrings. They're beautiful. I'm sure you don't mean any harm, I'm sure
you don't really think abt us at all. I'm sure you don't understand the
concept of off-limits. But what if by not wearing a headdress in yr music
video or changing yr damn mascot and perhaps adding .05% of personal
annoyance to yr life for the twenty minutes it lasts, the 103 young ppl
who tried to kill themselves on the Pine Ridge Indian reservation over
the past four months wanted to live 50% more

I don't want to be seen, generally, I'm a natural introvert, n I def don't
want to be seen by white ladies in buttery shawls,
but I will literally die if I don't scream

An NDN poem must reference alcoholism, like

I started drinking again after Mike Brown and Sandra Bland and Charleston
I felt so underwater it made no sense to keep dry

In my poem, I cdn't get out of bed for two days after Mike Brown and
Sandra Bland and Charleston

me n sweatpants n a new york slice

I feel dry as California
where I somehow managed to thrive in a climate of drought for thousands
of years w/o draining the state, yet somehow *we* were primitive?

Consequence shapes behavior. So does the absence of consequences.

America says *some ppl are raised guilty. Some are innocent of everything.*
Some ppl will always have to be good sports remain calm

Remain Calm

Remain Calm

Who even wants to go into space? I fucking hate traveling
I'm a weirdo NDN faggot and frankly that limits my prospects
plus it sucks—watching the couples and the string lights
slow-dance in Monbijoupark, to realize
despite history
my own abrupt American body

America that green ghost, been after me for at least a couple hundred
years somehow once convinced me to do its dirty work for it sharp in a
warm bath

Sun breaks upon the Pacific Northwest. Is this a nature poem again

At one point, there was a point. The air was still, I think. The sky was yellow at dusk and we were like cameos, flushed against the mountains.

Then there was lots of *stuff*. Like identifying with *pinole*. Like *the struggle*. Like *love*.

It's hard to unhook the heavy marble Nature from the chain around yr neck when history is stolen like water.

Reclamation suggests social

capital

In the opening poem of her book *Of Gods & Strangers*, Tina Chang writes, "As the trees split, a religion crashed to a moan./People were shocked to learn the sky was not a chariot of water."

America learned it scarcely rains in San Diego. Water was a battlefield and within just 20 years, from 1850 to 1870, the indigenous population fell by 60%

Look at all your family and friends

I am missing many cousins, have you seen them?

Anthropologists write "population decline" with the gentle implication of a drying fog. "Recourse" suggests resources. People say *get over*.

I read a lot. It's hard, but I'm starting to see the chariot of water.

No one told me abt "Space Oddity" by David Bowie

Everyone must feel fresh and weird, and perhaps rightly so
in the sense that yr the only one who has been you—
a slap in the face of squiggly sperm and probability

How cd u not feel like a miracle

in the sense that everyone in yr line had to survive primordial waves of
SoCal dehydration, waves of European disease, active predation by men
whose bullets were bought by the US government the pendulum of
genocidal legislation intended to rob yr tribe of it's sovereignty, the cultural
bleach of NDN boarding schools that robbed yr grandmother's generation
of the language, meth infestation of the 80s, and like George W. Bush

Ground Control really came around to Major Tom
and then loses him, like an orbit

Despite the flatness of the intro, I heard a ring of "traditional" motherly
concern in the first two lines, *take your protein pills and put yr helmet
on* vs the classical kind of detached father in the next line, *Check
ignition and may God's love be with you*

An explosion of belief from the skeptical Ground Control
after the rocket launch, how can you account for a spontaneous
recognition of talent
really floods the drum we call ear
and given the parental tint I heard in the beginning
I keep mishearing the soft lyric *tell my wife I love her very much*
to *tell my mom*

I tell the rez, *I think my spaceship knows which way to go*

I read abt shifting linguistics abt the extinction of such-and-such tribe
in so-and-so's novel in verse, a metaphor in the narrative of a dying
relationship

Metaphor, the traditional function of indigenous ppl in the grand
canon of lit

I look up from my trickle to the epochs above—

There's a line in the movie Smoke Signals, *the only thing more
pathetic than NDNs on TV is NDNs watching NDNs on TV* I cringe
at my cousin's dream catcher tattoo like bb that's not even our tribe
but I walked around for two whole lucid-ass years wearing bone
chokers wanting an artifact of my identity wanting life or death to
touch something of the rugged absence

Absence, as if Kumeyaay just didn't show up, as if it slept in, as if there
weren't a government intent on extermination

I'll never write a nature poem w/feather imagery or booze or that
describes a slow pocket of dew in a SoCal Feb AM

It was first a thrill
to see a tribe in those hugging pages
I took what I cd get

But now I see the night and she is dancing bird

It took tons

for me to come to this relationship

with even a thin crust mantle of optimism.

You say to yrself, into the mirror, the humidifier misting behind you—

Okay, first a selfie—

You say, *I'm going to do this. We're doing this.* Slipping into love like sleep.

What is it inside nature

that turns a color into danger,

a season into a reminder of sitting across each other across a tinny
table, copperish, unseasonably hot in our tall bodies no shade

while I waited

for the words I knew were coming.

Evolution is not very Victoria Beckham

is a thing I felt like saying

to myself on the subway ride home. And, *when will my neck finally be
long enough to reach the leaves
in the canopy?*

My singing teacher says, *just focus on yr breath.*

I don't know how to explain this next part, other than to say *I don't find breathing very relaxing, Pam.* Can't you see I'm trying super hard *not* to focus on my breath? I'm
trying to forget.

I look up at night thinking

and getting dizzy so I have to sit down

How many of you are there, up in the flat sky outside the city.

Vibrato is great on a lake with the doug firs pointing upwards, but I can't help it I miss the city. I miss the city when I'm in the city. Where *am* I?

That'ssssssss, okay, that's fine. Pam says. *Move to the country of yr breath,*

but you still have to sing the note, and the next
one and the next.

Nature kisses me outside the movie theater

I can't tell if it was a romantic comedy or a scary movie bc of politics

When Nature palms my neck I can't tell if it's a romantic comedy or a
scary movie bc the clarity of desire terrifies me like a stage
comfort only leads to predation, and anything marvelous
becomes holy in the Google translate of humanity

I prefer to keep it very doggy style

bc holy roars untouchable, tempers flare
and ppl die, violently, all over the world throughout time

The difference btwn me at 15 and me now is being called a faggot was
humiliating bc I thought faggotry was hot, sulfuric garbage

but now in the arclight of a self not unmade by shame, tho the
violence is scary w/this pale brawny NYU shithead callin us faggots,
the sentiment sounds more like ice
clinkin in a tumbler of vodka lemonade

Who dis?

You can't be an NDN person in today's world

and write a nature poem. I swore to myself I would never write a nature
poem. Let's be clear, I hate nature—hate its *guts*

I say to my audience. There is something smaller I say to myself:

I don't hate nature at all. Places have thoughts—hills have backs that love
being stroked by our eyes. The river gobbles down its tract as a metaphor
but also abt its day. The bluffs purr when we put down blankets at the
downturn of the sun and laugh at a couple on a obvi OkCupid date

and even more stellar, the jellybean moon sugars at me. She flies and
beams and I breathe.

Fuck that. I recant. I slap myself.

Let's say I live in NYC. Let's say I was the first person in my family to
graduate college. Let's say UGH I like watching *New Girl* on Hulu.

This is the difference:

Some see objects in the Earth, where I see lungs. Sky mother falls thru
a hole, lands on a turtle.

Hole is my favorite band.

Body

of text is the Lazarus
a deathless tablet, the Enheduanna

like a Freddy or a Jason?
Won't stay dead

No, weirdo.
We r suggesting the vigor lives
like horror, but it's opposite. You also inherit the strengths of yr lineage.

What survives is improbable. What claps back is a miracle.

What if a poem was just the interpretation?

No, no. Put yr shirt back on.

We compare hand sizes in bed I say *I just want to be on the same page*

You are one person with me, and someone different by yourself—here,
you can be with me and by yourself at the same
time. *How are we doing?*

"Fast Car" by Tracy Chapman is literally the best song in human history. It's one of those songs where, u listen to other songs n yr like . . . *these are all crap*. Everything I read, listen to, and see is reminding me of "Fast Car" by Tracy Chapman rn.

Repeating patterns, the mistakes of yr parents, running but not getting very far. Not as far as you wanted but maybe farther than you think. In the beginning she's like *let's take yr fast car and get out of here*. Then they live together and she's like *let's get away from our . . . domestic issues . . . by taking a ride in yr fast car* (feeling tethered to a feature can really keep ppl in a shitty situation). And then at the very end she's like yr a drunk and you take yr fast car and get the fuck out of here.

How far can you actually get away from the bases?

Body

Let's never go to Vegas
k?
Body let's never talk
to those who feel nothing
in front of neon signs,
or those who talk
abt how death is the only perfection.

Are we confronting thots, or pushing them aside? I want to fuck

Hey, I remember the 90s
I was friends with the 90s
I had anxiety in the 90s

I remember hearing Princess Di died on the radio not knowing who
she was but my mother was weirdly devastated talking abt it to the
paramedics carrying away my auntie

To be comfortable in your cement is a miracle. It hugs,
it feels like a voice. A voice has skin. I am looking at the stars on the
sea. Let's never go go

There's no such thing as a perfect ending. You just have to stand up
and say, *I'm ready to leave.*

When a star dies, it becomes any number of things
like a black hole, or a documentary.

The early universe of our skin was remarkably smooth
now I stand in a rapidly dampening Christina Aguilera tee

The first stars were born of a gravity, my ancestors—
our sky is really the only thing same for me as it was for them,
which is a pretty stellar inheritance

I don't know how they made sense of that swell, how they survived long
enough to make me, and am sort of at war with sentimentality, generally

but that absence of an answer, yet suggestion of meaning
isn't ultimately that different from a poem
So I've started reading the stars

Nothing is possible until it happens, like digesting sulfur instead of sunlight
or friends with benefits

Poems were my scripture and the poets, my gods
but even gods I mean especially gods are subject to the artifice
of humanity.

I look up at the poem, all of them up there in the hot sky and fall
into the water, a stone

What if I really do feel connected to the land?

What if the mountains around the valley where I was born

What if I see them like faces when I close my eyes

What if I said hi to them in the mornings and now all their calls go to voicemail

What if I would ride my big wheels down the drive too fast headfirst into the chaparral and I'd steal myself from them scratchy having felt the pulse

What if I said *sorry* under my breath when I sat on moss on the rock at the crick behind myself

I would look like a freaking moron basket case

I get so disappointed by stupid NDNs writing their dumb nature poems like grow up faggots

I look this thought full in the face and want to throw myself into traffic

Admit it. This is the poem you wanted all along.

It's hard to be anything

but a pessimist

when you feel the Earth rotting away on so many home pages and Taylor
Swift is an idiot and cigarettes
cost an arm and a leg

I'm on a porch petting kitties and there is lavender in the air. The sun
is over the hill and my friend Roy knows the names of all the plants in
his front yard. One of the kitties is named Witch Baby and she likes to
perch around your neck.

The air is clear, and all across Instagram—peeps are posting pics of
the sunset.

ACKNOWLEDGEMENTS:

Excerpts from this poem have appeared in *Apogee, No Tokens, Fanzine, Western Beefs of North America, Familiars Quarterly, Imperial Matters, the Offing, 429 Magazine, Cosmonauts Avenue, Pinwheel, Public Pool, the Washington Square Review, the Felt, Tin House, February: an Anthology, Hobart, 90's Meg Ryan, Glittermob, Out Magazine, Ocho, Hello Mr.,* and *New York Tyrant*

Shout out to Matthew, Tony, and the whole Tin House team for letting me get my way most of the time. Thanks to Roy Pérez, on whose couch I wrote the original 23-page zine version of this book, to Morgan Parker who sent the final manuscript to Tin House, and to everyone who gave me stage time in between to work out the "material." Thanks again to Cat Glennon for the beautiful book cover, Lauren Wilkinson for our writing dates, and the Kumeyaay nation for incubating me.

TOMMY "TEEBS" PICO is a poet, podcaster, and TV writer. The winner of a 2018 Whiting Award, he is the author of the books *IRL*, *Nature Poem*, *Junk*, *Feed*, and the zine series *Hey, Teebs*. Originally from the Viejas Indian reservation of the Kumeyaay nation, he now splits his time between Los Angeles and Brooklyn. He co-curates the reading series Poets with Attitude, co-hosts the podcasts *Food 4 Thot* and *Scream, Queen!*, is poetry editor at Catapult Magazine, writes on the TV shows *Reservation Dogs* and *Resident Alien*, and is a contributing editor at Literary Hub.

@heyteebs

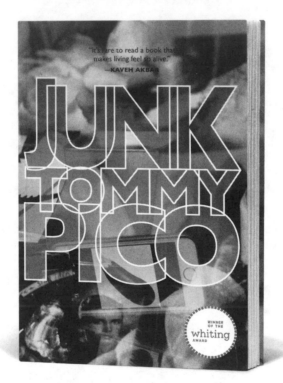